I0172951

Discipleship Series

ADVENTURES INTO
New Beginnings with Jesus Christ

Ebenezer & Abigail
Gabriels

Ebenezer & Abigail Gabriels
IAUC Institute.com

www.EbenezerGabriels.Org
hello@ebenezergabriels.org

DEDICATION

To Jesus, the Root and Offspring of David
The Redeemer and the Author of Our Faith
The One who died so we don't have to die
The One who lives forever and ever

CONTENT

1   The Lost Soul   Pg 7

2   Divine Exchange   Pg 14

3   New Beginnings   Pg 19

4   A New Companion &   Pg 24
    Friend - The Holy
    Spirit

5   The Forming of   Pg 32
    Christ in You

6   Growing in Jesus   Pg 37
    Christ

7   Excelling in Faith   Pg 46

8   Finishing Strong   Pg 52

1

~

THE LOST SOUL

On the day you were created, before your flesh was created, God made your soul, and He wrote your purpose in life into your soul as seen in Psalm 139: 16 *Your eyes saw my substance, being yet unformed. And in Your book they all were written, The days fashioned for me, When as yet there were none of them.* After creating you, He then placed you in your mother's womb, and gave you the breath of life to come to the world to manifest His purpose in your lifetime.

When many came on earth, they lost connection to the Lord God who is the Owner of all souls, and handed over their soul to the devil, allowing him to drive their soul into perdition. Any soul that has been captured by the devil is under the danger of hell, except the soul is redeemed just as the Lord spoke through the mouth of Prophetic in Ezekiel 18:4 *"Behold, all souls are Mine; The soul of the*

Father, as well as the soul of the son, is Mine; The soul who sins shall die.

A soul without Christ is a lost soul held in the captivity of darkness.

Here are some indicators of a lost soul listed below:

- A life not given to Jesus Christ.
- Sinful living
- Filthiness in thoughts
- Consulting idols, mediums and spiritist
- Practicing witchcraft and sorcery
- False religion, or religion without a relationship with the Lord
- Occult and rituals
- Unholy living
- and all types of the works of the flesh

Revelation 21:8 continues with the listing of fleshly activities and manifestations of a soul captured by the devil: *the cowardly, unbelieving, abominable, murderers, sexually immoral, sorcerers, idolaters, and all liars shall have their part in the lake which burns with fire and brimstone, which is the second death."*

THE MANY TROUBLES OF A LOST SOUL
- A lost soul never enjoys the freedom in Jesus.
- A lost soul is continually oppressed with the rod of men.

- A lost soul remains in all forms of slavery - mental slavery, emotional slavery, financial slavery, and spiritual slavery.
- A lost soul continues to offer sacrifices with the blood of goats, blood of chicken, blood of cow, and all forms of rituals
- A lost soul goes from trouble into another series of afflictions.
- A lost soul is continually oppressed by the forces of darkness.
- A lost soul continues to feast at satanic tables of darkness.
- A lost soul remains under the bondage of satanic priests and satanic prophets.
- A lost soul seeks to mix the worship of other gods with the true worship of the Living God.
- A lost soul is a fugitive on the earth, never walking into their inheritance or discovering their purpose.
- A lost soul continues to remain unrepentant
- A lost soul ends up in the lake of fire according to Revelation 21:8.

THE MIGHTY GOD: THE GOD OF JUSTICE AND MERCY
All people on earth have sinned, and there is no one without sin. God is a God of Justice as revealed in Ezekiel 18:4, *"Behold, all souls are Mine; The soul of the father as well as the soul of the son is Mine; The soul who sins shall die.*

The mercy of the Lord has also given a way out of the wrath of His anger in judgment. This is why He said through the Prophet in Isaiah 1:8 *Come now, and let us* reason together," Says the Lord, "Though your sins are like scarlet, They shall be as white as snow; Though they are red like crimson, They shall be as wool. If you are willing and obedient, You shall eat the good of the land. The only way to obtain the mercy of the Lord is through Jesus Christ.

MAKING A DECISION TO COME TO THE LORD JESUS

Regardless of how dark the past was, there is an ordinance of God that cancels the debt of the past as written in 2 Corinthians 5:17 *Therefore, if anyone is in Christ, he is a new creation; old things have passed away; behold, all things have become new.*

To come to Jesus, you need to *confess with your mouth the Lord Jesus and believe in your heart that God has raised Him from the dead, you will be saved* - Romans 10:9.

PRAYERS FOR THE SALVATION OF YOUR SOUL TO SECURE YOUR ETERNITY WITH JESUS

Lord Jesus, I come to you just the way I am, as a sinner, lost without hope, have mercy on me. I acknowledged that you died for me, your blood was shed in place of mine, and you resurrected to sit on the right hand side of the Living God. Please forgive me, I forsake all other gods. Lord Jesus, cleanse me with your blood, make atonement for my sin. I acknowledge that you are now my Lord and Savior, and you are the Son of the Living God. Establish me in my new life in you, and open up the revelation of how to worship you, Lord, in Jesus' Name I pray.

KEEPING YOUR SALVATION
1. Depart from old ways of iniquity.
2. You must be baptized in the Holy Spirit.
3. Learn about Jesus through the Word of God.
4. Become a deep worshipper of Yahweh.
5. Know that salvation is the greatest form of deliverance, and is a lifelong journey
6. Grow in the faith by fellowshipping with other believers.
7. Have a goal of heaven in mind.

Discipleship: New beginnings with Jesus Christ

12

NOTES

2

~

DIVINE EXCHANGE

Your salvation was costly. It cost the blood of the only son of God. As seen in the Old Testament, the Scriptures tell us about the divine exchange where the blood of Jesus was used to make atonement for our sins and the purchase of our souls.

THE POWER OF BLOOD

The life of every animal, including humans, is in the blood. The bible speaks about this mystery.

> For the life of the flesh is in the blood, and I have given it to you upon the altar to make atonement for your souls; for it is the blood that makes atonement for the soul.' - Leviticus 17:11

The blood is so powerful, that the Lord mandated the priests in the old testament to make atonement for community sins through the blood of animals.

RULES ON THE FORGIVENESS OF SIN

Without an atonement, it is impossible to receive forgiveness, as seen in Hebrews 9:22. *And according to the law, almost all things are purified with blood, and without shedding of blood there is no remission.*

THE BLOOD OF JESUS

Jesus Christ came to put an end to the use of blood and rituals for the atonement of sins, as seen in Hebrews 9:11-14. *But Christ came as High Priest of the good things to come, with the greater and more perfect tabernacle not made with hands, that is, not of this creation. Not with the blood of goats and calves, but with His blood He entered the Most Holy Place once for all, having obtained eternal redemption. For if the blood of bulls and goats and the ashes of a heifer, sprinkling the unclean, sanctifies for the purifying of the flesh, how much more shall the blood of Christ, who through the eternal Spirit offered Himself without spot to God, cleanse your conscience from dead works to serve the living God?* Since the blood of Jesus had been shed for our sins, we are no longer required to make atonement of any type because the blood of Jesus has satisfied this requirement.

As a new believer, you should know that the blood of Jesus is very precious and should not be abused. There is also great power in the blood of Jesus.

PRAYERS TO DECREE THE BLOOD OF JESUS

WORSHIP DECREE
Life for life,
Blood for blood
Divine exchange
That's what you did for me
I'm forever grateful, forever blessed
Your life in place of mine.

MEDIDATE
Revelation 5:9

> And they sang a new song, saying: "You are worthy to take the scroll, And to open its seals; For You were slain, And have redeemed us to God by Your blood Out of every tribe and tongue and people and nation..

PRAYER TO DECREE THE BLOOD OF JESUS OVER ALL SITUATIONS
1. Lord Jesus, thank you for the provision in the blood of Jesus.
2. Lord Jesus, let your blood be my covering in the name of Jesus.
3. Lord Jesus, let your blood wash clean my foundation, in the name of Jesus.
4. Lord Jesus, let the blood of Jesus cleanse every iniquity in my life in the name of Jesus.

5. Lord, let the blood of Jesus redeem my household in the name of Jesus.
6. I am dedicated to the Lord through the blood of Jesus.
7. Let the eyes of my understanding be enlightened by the blood of Jesus.

NOTES

3

~

NEW BEGINNINGS

A Christian is someone who believes and has confessed with their mouth that "Jesus is Lord". *Romans 10:9 notes that if you confess with your mouth the Lord Jesus and believe in your heart that God has raised Him from the dead, you will be saved.* The only requirement to becoming a Christian is to acknowledge your sinful ways, forsake your old ways of sin, and confess the Lordship of Jesus over your life, which you did in Chapter One. A new life in Christ means you are now a follower of Jesus Christ, and you live your life in submission to the teachings and directions of Jesus Christ as seen in the Scripture.

EMBRACE THE NEW JOURNEY AND THE NEW LIFE.

The old man that you once were led to destruction. The new man has a destination of eternal life. The old man grows into corruption, while the new life grows into corruption.

Your new life began when you said YES to Jesus. This means you now live differently. You will be putting away the old lifestyles and taking off the old garments. You are taking off all the former conducts and putting up a Christ-like garment.

Becoming a Christian means you are now a follower of Jesus, and you will love Him with your mind, heart, and soul. As a new Christian, this book will help you understand the grace of salvation that has just been released to you. The book also takes you on a study of new beginnings after salvation. It is what it means to give one's life to Christ. You have opened the bag of mystery into what it means to be a child of God.

Whenever a new believer gives their life to Christ, it is a journey into newness which is continued until the day of perfection. It is a new journey into the heart of the Father. It is a journey that only begins with a step of saying "I do" to the Bridegroom. It is the opening up of the bank of mystery of the kingdom of God. It is the opening up of the mysteries of who God is.

PRAYERS FOR THE BELIEVER'S FOUNDATION

WORSHIP DECREE
Life for life,
Blood for blood
Divine exchange
That's what you did for me
I'm forever grateful, forever blessed
Your life in place of mine.

MEDIDATE
Isaiah 9:2-7

> The people who walked in darkness. Have seen a great light; Those who dwelt in the land of the shadow of death, Upon them a light has shined. You have multiplied the nation And increased its joy; They rejoice before You. According to the joy of harvest, As men rejoice when they divide the spoil. For You have broken the yoke of his burden And the staff of his shoulder, The rod of his oppressor, As in the day of Midian. For every warrior's sandal from the noisy battle, And garments rolled in blood, Will be used for burning and fuel of fire.For unto us a Child is born, Unto us a Son is given; And the government will be upon His shoulder. And His name will be called Wonderful, Counselor, Mighty God, Everlasting Father, Prince of Peace. Of the increase of His government and peace There will be no end, Upon the throne of David and over His

kingdom, To order it and establish it with judgment and justice From that time forward, even forever. The zeal of the Lord of hosts will perform this.

PRAYER OF THE FOUNDATION FOR THE NEW BELIEVER IN JESUS CHRIST

8. Lord Jesus, show me great and mighty things in the name of Jesus.
9. My Lord, thank you for the power of your deliverance in the name of Jesus.
10. My Lord, my Father, clothe me with the garment of righteousness in the name of Jesus.
11. Thou spirit of iniquity, be uprooted from my foundation in the name of Jesus
12. My Lord, clothe me with the garment of holiness in the name of Jesus
13. All spirits of lethargy that want to put me to slumber, be cast out of my life in the name of Jesus.
14. Lord, deliver me from the idolatry in my foundation, in the name of Jesus
15. My Lord and my Father, I will give praise to Your holy name in the name of Jesus
16. Cast out all forms of pollution in the name of Jesus
17. Pollution in my soul, be flushed out by the blood of Jesus

NOTES

4

~

A NEW COMPANION & FRIEND - THE HOLY SPIRIT.

The world is a very complicated place. It is a vast place, and Jesus knew this because He lived as a human just like you and I thousands of years ago. Before He departed this world, He prayed to the Lord to send us a helper, which is the Holy Spirit. In your new walk with the Lord, you have a new friend, a helper, and a companion in the Holy Spirit of God. The moment you gave your life to Jesus Christ, you were baptized in the name of Jesus, and a gift of the Holy Spirit has been released unto you. *Then Peter said to them, "Repent, and let every one of you be baptized in the name of Jesus Christ for the remission of sins; and you shall receive the gift of the Holy Spirit. - Acts 2:38*

THE ROLE OF THE HOLY SPIRIT IN THE LIFE OF THE BELIEVER

The Holy Spirit is Your New Helper
The Holy Spirit will teach you spiritual lessons, deeper things from the presence of the Lord.

> *But the Helper, the Holy Spirit, whom the Father will send in My name, He will teach you all things, and bring to your remembrance all things that I said to you - John 14:28*

The Holy Spirit will remind you the teachings of Jesus in the Scriptures, the Holy Spirit will also show you the right way so that you will not stumble in your walk

The Holy Spirit Resides in Your Body
Your body is no longer yours. It has been taken back from the devil and now the temple of God, where the Holy Spirit resides.

> *Or do you not know that your body is the temple of the Holy Spirit who is in you, whom you have from God, and you are not your own? - 1 Corinthians 6:19*

Growth Tips:
1. The presence of the Holy Spirit in your life is to be highly valued. This is why you should embrace and make a life of holiness your focus, and stay away from appearances of sin. You can not conquer sin by yourself, but through the power of the Holy Spirit.
2. It is important that all sins, including adultery, fornication, gossip and all forms of worldliness

3. When we speak in tongues, we speak in an encoded language to God that only the Lord understands.

The Holy Spirit Teaches You How to pray

Prayer is a spiritual exercise. The Holy Spirit will guide you in your prayer life.

> *Likewise the Spirit also helps in our weaknesses. For we do not know what we should pray for as we ought, but the Spirit Himself makes intercession for us with groanings which cannot be uttered.* - Romans 8:26

Growth Tips:
1. The Lord will release the gift of tongues unto you as you continue to fellowship, and you will speak in new tongues powered by the Holy Spirit.
2. When we speak in tongues, we speak in an encoded language to God that only the Lord understands

The Holy Spirit Will Tell You What the Lord Says
The Holy Spirit will tell you what the Lord says, and reveal deep and secret things unto you.

> *However, when He, the Spirit of truth, has come, He will guide you into all truth; for He will not speak on His authority, but whatever He hears He will speak; and He will tell you things to come.* - John 16:13

The Holy Spirit will teach you if you are a student studying in school. The Holy Spirit will teach you if you are a professional. The Holy Spirit will warn you if there are impending dangers. The Holy Spirit will show you the direction in which you should go.

Growth Tips:
1. To benefit from the Holy Spirit, you must embrace obedience. The Holy Spirit does not enforce obedience; however, there is great joy and life in obedience.
2. You must learn to grow in the maturity of the Holy Spirit so you can understand perfectly how the Holy Spirit speaks to you.

The Holy Spirit Teaches How to Speak.
As a new believer, your words and speech will be guided by the Holy Spirit.

> For the *Holy Spirit* will teach you in that very hour what you ought to say." Luke 12:12

Your words will be the words of the Holy Spirit. Your words will be approved by the Lord. No more pulling others down through negative speech, but the Holy Spirit will take over your speech, and you will build others up with words of life.

THE NEW BELIEVER'S PRAYERS FOR THE POWER OF THE HOLY SPIRIT

WORSHIP DECREES
Let Your blood atone for me,
Let Your oil flow on my head
Let Your fire set my altars ablaze
Let Your wind blow over my soul
Let Your spirit fill me up
Let Your spirit be my companion

MEDIDATE
Have mercy upon me, O God,
According to Your lovingkindness;
According to the multitude of Your tender mercies,
Blot out my transgressions.
Wash me thoroughly from my iniquity,
And cleanse me from my sin.
For I acknowledge my transgressions,
And my sin is always before me.
Against You, You only, have I sinned,
And done this evil in Your sight—
That You may be found just when You speak,
And blameless when You judge.
Behold, I was brought forth in iniquity,
And in sin my mother conceived me.
6Behold, You desire truth in the inward parts,
And in the hidden part You will make me to know wisdom.

Purge me with hyssop, and I shall be clean;
Wash me, and I shall be whiter than snow.
Make me hear joy and gladness,
That the bones You have broken may rejoice.
Hide Your face from my sins,
And blot out all my iniquities.
Create in me a clean heart, O God,
And renew a steadfast spirit within me.
Do not cast me away from Your presence,
And do not take Your Holy Spirit from me.
Restore to me the joy of Your salvation,
And uphold me by Your generous Spirit.
Then I will teach transgressors Your ways,
And sinners shall be converted to You.
Deliver me from the guilt of bloodshed, O God,
The God of my salvation,
And my tongue shall sing aloud of Your righteousness.
O Lord, open my lips,
And my mouth shall show forth Your praise.
For You do not desire sacrifice, or else I would give it;
You do not delight in burnt offering.
The sacrifices of God are a broken spirit,
A broken and a contrite heart—
These, O God, You will not despise.
Do good in Your good pleasure to Zion;
Build the walls of Jerusalem.
Then You shall be pleased with the sacrifices of righteousness, With burnt offering and whole burnt offering;
Then they shall offer bulls on Your altar.

PRAYER FOR BAPTISM OF THE HOLY SPIRIT

1. I shall no longer be cut off from the power of the Holy Spirit, in the name of Jesus
2. I received the baptism of the Holy Spirit in the name of Jesus
3. I receive the fire of the Holy Spirit in the name of Jesus.
4. Lord, let the fire of the Holy Spirit go into my foundation, to burn every chaff of darkness in the name of Jesus.
5. Lord, open my eyes to your revelation in the name of Jesus
6. Lord, let my spirit be tuned to the broadcast of heaven in the name of Jesus
7. Lord, let my ears be opened to your revelation in the name of Jesus

NOTES

5

~

THE FORMING OF CHRIST IN YOU

When a new believer converts, they begin a new journey of Jesus forming up in them. As Jesus is formed in the new believer, the new believer begins to take on the image of Jesus, and the power of God comes upon them.

WHAT YOU NEED TO KNOW ABOUT JESUS CHRIST FORMING IN YOU

#1. YOU ARE NOW BORN AGAIN

As a new believer, you are like a newborn baby in the Spirit, and you should desire to grow in Christ. The Scripture helps us understand that - *My little children, for whom I labor in birth again until Christ is formed in you - Galatians 4:19*

#2. GROWING WITH THE BABY MILK

Your growth in Jesus begins with feeding on the milk of the Spirit, which is the word of God. The word of God develops you and helps you grow - *as newborn babes, desire the pure milk of the word, that you may grow thereby* - *1 Peter 2:2*

#3. YOU ARE NOT YOUR OWN

When you gave your life to Christ, your flesh died and you no longer live, but Jesus now lives in you.

> *I have been crucified with Christ; it is no longer I who live, but Christ lives in me; and the life which I now live in the flesh I live by faith in the Son of God, who loved me and gave Himself for me.- Galatians 2:20*

#4. GET TO KNOW JESUS.

As a groom and bride are excited to know about each other, you will grow by seeking more knowledge of Jesus. Jesus is the Son of God. He died for our sins. The Scripture gives us a deeper understanding of the life of Jesus.

> *But grow in the grace and knowledge of our Lord and Savior Jesus Christ. To him be glory both now and forever! Amen. 2 Peter 2:18*

Growth Tips:

- As a new believer, Jesus is your model. He is the perfect example. His life shows us how to live life and how to handle all the situations we encounter. There is victory over all powers of darkness when the new believer embraces Jesus and lives like Him.

- Learn about Jesus through the Scripture, and the image of Jesus will be revealed to you.
- Join small Bible study groups where you study the Word together and learn from the experiences of other believers.
- Learn about the ministry of Jesus by reading the books of John, Matthew, and Mark.
- Identify your purpose (*Unprofaned Purpose Bible Study Book by Ebenezer Gabriels & Abigail Gabriels*)
- Learn what worship means and how to cultivate a life of worship by reading the first book of the Bible and also the book of John.
- Learn about the principles of revelation, and growing in hearing from God
- Learn about the gifts of the Holy Spirit by reading the books of 1 and 2nd Corinthians and the book of Acts
- Learn about discernment of spirits and grow in the gifts of your spirit.
- Learn about spiritual warfare by reading the book of Daniel. (*Additional Recommended readings Uncursed Purpose Bible Study Book by Ebenezer Gabriels & Abigail Gabriels*)

PRAYERS OF READINESS AS CHRIST IS FORMED IN YOU

WORSHIP DECREES

Let Your blood atone for me,
Let Your oil flow on my head
Let Your fire set my altars ablaze
Let Your wind blow over my soul
Let Your spirit fill me up
Let Your spirit be my companion

MEDIDATE

Now thanks be to God who always leads us in triumph in Christ, and through us diffuses the fragrance of His knowledge in every place - II Corinthians 2:14

PRAYER FOR GROWTH IN THE KNOWLEDGE OF JESUS

1. Father, I thank you Lord for the grace made available by the blood of Jesus
2. My Lord, let your Holy Spirit advance your works in my life in the name of Jesus
3. Father, baptize me with the power of the holy Spirit in the name of Jesus
4. Jesus Christ, grow in me in the name of Jesus
5. I shall not limit the growth of Jesus in my life in the name of Jesus
6. Father, let my mind be tuned to yours as you reveal the glory of the Lord to me in the name of Jesus.

7. Let the knowledge of Jesus manifest in me in Jesus' Name.

NOTES

6

~

GROWING IN JESUS CHRIST

Growth never stops for the new believer. There is something new to learn every day. The Scripture teaches you everything you need to learn

> *Therefore let us move beyond the elementary teachings about Christ and be taken forward to maturity, not laying again the foundation of repentance from acts that lead to death, and of faith in God - Hebrews 6:1*

#1. BECOMING A PART OF THE BODY OF CHRIST
As a believer, you are now a part of the body the Christ.

For just as the body is one and has many members, and all the members of the body, though many, are one body, so it is with Christ. For in one Spirit we were all baptized into one body—Jews or Greeks, slaves or free—and all were made to drink of one Spirit. For the body does not consist of one member but of many. If the foot should say, "Because I am not a hand, I do not belong to the body," that would not make it any less a part of the body. And if the ear should say, "Because I am not an eye, I do not belong to the body," that would not make it any less a part of the body.

The gathering of people submitted to Jesus as Lord and Savior is called the Church. This gathering is the family of Jesus on earth. The Church is the bride of Jesus on earth.

And He is the head of the body, the church, who is the beginning, the firstborn from the dead, that in all things He may have the preeminence - Colossians 1:18.

The Holy Spirit backed Church is the foundation of all teachings of truth and training of believers. The church is also a place where the power of the Holy Spirit develops the spiritual, mental, and all types of giftings.

Now you are the body of Christ, and members individually. And God has appointed these in the church: first apostles, second prophets, third teachers, after that miracles, then gifts of healings, helps, administrations, varieties of tongues. Are all apostles? Are All prophets? Are all teachers? Are all workers of miracles? Do all have gifts of healings? Do all speak with tongues? Do all interpret? But earnestly desire the best gifts. And yet I show you a more excellent way.

Body of Jesus Christ Tips:
1. Every new believer must be aligned with a church of God on earth.
2. It is important that a new believer finds a Biblically-grounded church filled with the Holy Spirit to become a part of the body of Jesus Christ here on earth.
3. Do not be in a hurry to join a church because everyone is attending. Many houses of the devil are now disguised as churches.
4. Prayerfully ask the Holy Spirit in you to show you the Church where God's presence is.

What is a Church and How to Find a Real Church?

A church is not a building; it is the coming together of two or three people, whether in your house, your friend's house, in a library, at a cafeteria, a group, or even in a sanctuary building, or even in a virtual group.

The early church was characterized by the gathering of believers in their homes, in the upper room, and in small groups where each person had the opportunity to grow, serve, and thrive in faith.

Acts 2:42-47
42 They devoted themselves to the apostles' teaching and to fellowship, to the breaking of bread and to prayer. 43

Everyone was filled with awe at the many wonders and signs performed by the apostles. 44 All the believers were together and had everything in common. 45 They sold property and possessions to give to anyone who had need. 46 Every day they continued to meet together in the temple courts. They broke bread in their homes and ate together with glad and sincere hearts, 47 praising God and enjoying the favor of all the people. And the Lord added to their number daily those who were being saved.

The early church was characterized by the gathering of believers in their homes, in the upper room, and in small groups where each person had the opportunity to grow, serve, and thrive in faith.

#2. GROWING IN THE LOVE OF JESUS

The love of God is the foundation of our salvation through Jesus Christ. We were sinners, and then God sent Jesus to come and take up our sins upon Himself. Such great love!.

> *And He is the head of the body, the church, who is the beginning, the firstborn from the dead, that in all things He may have the preeminence* - Colossians 1:18.

The Holy Spirit backed Church is the foundation of all teachings of truth and training of believers. The church is also a place where the power of the Holy Spirit develops the spiritual, mental, and all types of giftings.

Loving Jesus Tips:

1. One of the ways to love Jesus is to keep His word. Follow His teachings and receive his instructions.
2. Make friends with the Scripture, read and read and read again. This is the Only Way to get the revelation of Jesus Christ.

#3. GROWING IN THE FELLOWSHIP OF JESUS

New believers should seek to associate with other believers of Jesus Christ, whether in their communities or even in online forums. This will strengthen you in your walk with the Lord. In fellowship, believers grow in their faith and understanding of the Scriptures and the ministry of Jesus.

> *Do not be unequally yoked together with unbelievers. For what fellowship has righteousness with lawlessness? And what communion has light with darkness? - II Corinthians 6:14*

Fellowship Tips:
1. Fellowship with the wrong associations can become a snare for believers.
2. Fellowship in the wrong groups can lure the well-intending believers away from the Lord's presence.
3. Fellowship must be Christ-centered, and all about Jesus, nothing short.

THE NEW BELIEVER'S PRAYERS FOR GROWTH IN CHRIST

WORSHIP DECREES
Let Your blood atone for me,
Let Your oil flow on my head
Let Your fire set my altars ablaze
Let Your wind blow over my soul
Let Your spirit fill me up
Let Your spirit be my companion

MEDIDATE
Now thanks be to God who always leads us in triumph in Christ, and through us diffuses the fragrance of His knowledge in every place – II Corinthians 2:14

PRAYER FOR GROWTH IN THE KNOWLEDGE OF JESUS
1. My Lord, let your power overshadow me in the name of Jesus
2. My Lord, let the revelation of Jesus be made known to me in the name of Jesus.
3. Lord, let your light shine into all dark areas of my life in the name of Jesus.
4. Lord, feed me in your word in the name of Jesus
5. I shall not be cut short in my journey of salvation in Jesus name
6. Let the gates of my heart be opened to the teaching of the Lord Jesus, in Jesus name

7. Lord, deception shall not creep into my heart in the name of Jesus.

8. My Lord, let me surrender fully to the Lord Jesus in the name of Jesus.

NOTES

7

~

EXCELLING IN FAITH

Excelling in faith means you are progressing in your walk with the Lord. Growing began when you gave your life to Jesus, but you should focus on continuous growth into a spiritual house of Christ as the Scripture teaches: *Coming to Him as to a living stone, rejected indeed by men, but chosen by God and precious, you also, as living stones, are being built up a spiritual house, a holy priesthood, to offer up spiritual sacrifices acceptable to God through Jesus Christ - 1 Peter 2:4-5*

As a new believer, do not be ignorant of the tactics of the devil. Satan is always seeking to snatch you away from God's presence. He seeks to steal the salvation of people and lure them back onto the path of hell. If you are focused on excelling in your faith, satan becomes powerless over his attempts to derail you.

GROWING IN THE WORD OF GOD

As a new believer, you will begin to access different levels of revelation as you begin to dive deeper into God's word. There are different levels in your walk with the Lord, which is accessible as you grow in the word of word. The more you grow in His word, the more of God's revelation you have. As you grow into God's word, you will experience maturity through some of the following manifestations in your life.

1. You come into the realization of the fact that Jesus loves you, and His grace made available for you His blood
2. Death to the works of the flesh in your life
3. Entering and understanding of spiritual warfare
4. Entering into God's presence through the depth of worship and living a life of complete worship,

PREPARING TO EXCEL IN YOUR FAITH

As you excel, find a church or ministry to fellowship and to serve.
- Read the Bible everyday
- Become a worshipper of the Lord
- Seek the Lord and grow in spiritual gifts
- Live a fasted lifestyle
- Make friends with like-minded Christians who can help your faith
- Cultivate a strong prayer lifestyle
- Desire the gifts of speaking in tongues
- Build your spiritual senses
- Under spiritual warfare
- Live a life of obedience to the Lord
- Join a ministry in church

- Worship ministry
- Intercession ministry
- Bible Study Group
- Prophetic ministry

Overall, the believer who seeks to excel must strive for personal growth in their walk with the Lord.

Need help with starting afresh in Jesus christ?

PRAYERS FOR EXCELLENCE IN FAITH

WORSHIP DECREES
Let Your blood atone for me,
Let Your oil flow on my head
Let Your fire set my altars ablaze
Let Your wind blow over my soul
Let Your spirit fill me up
Let Your spirit be my companion

MEDIDATE
I Peter 2:5

> *you also, as living stones, are being built up a spiritual house, a holy priesthood, to offer up spiritual sacrifices acceptable to God through Jesus Christ.*

PRAYER FOR EXCELING IN THE WALK WITH GOD

1. My Lord, thank you for showing me deep and secret things in the name of Jesus.
2. Lord and Savior, thank you for the power in your Word, in the name of Jesus
3. I shall not be fruitless in my walk with you.
4. Build me up as your spiritual warrior in the name of Jesus.
5. Lord, open up a new level of your revelation to me today in Jesus' name
6. Jesus, my Great Teacher, teach me deeper things of the spirit in the name of Jesus

7. Chains of idolatry in my foundation, pulling me back from excelling, let the fire of the Holy Ghost burn you to ashes in the name of Jesus.
8. Spirit of religion holding me back from excelling in Christ, catch fire in the name of Jesus.
9. The spirit of demotion shall not pull me back into my old life in the name of Jesus.
10. I shall not meet with faith killers in the name of Jesus
11. I shall not meet with satanic priests in the name of Jesus.
12. Lord, bring me into a place of excellence in you in Jesus name.

NOTES

8

~

FINISHING STRONG

As a new believer, it is important to put the goal of reigning with Jesus Christ in eternity in view and at the center of your new life. While there are the promises of deliverance, prosperity, power, and great rewards available through Jesus Christ for those who seek it, the focus on heaven should not be lost.

VICTORY FOR FINISHING STRONG

At the end of the life of every believer, they should be able to look back and say - I *have fought the good fight, I have finished the race, I have kept the faith* - II Timothy 4:7. Victory is assured to the believer if the believer finishes strong.

Critical to reigning with Christ is finishing strong after salvation. Ezekiel 18:24 notes, "*But when a righteous man turns away from his righteousness and commits iniquity, and does according to all the abominations that the wicked man does, shall he live? All the righteousness which he has done shall not be remembered; because of the unfaithfulness of which he is guilty and the sin which he has committed, because of them he shall die.*

SPIRITUAL VIOLENCE REQUIRED TO ENTER INTO THE KINGDOM OF GOD

This is why it is important not to be derailed, and continue to live a life of worship. Jesus, while on earth told his disciples in Matthew 11: 12 how difficult it is to enter into the kingdom of God in heaven, He said, "*And from the days of John the Baptist until now the kingdom of heaven suffers violence, and the violent take it by force*".

THE HEAVENLY GIFT : THE CROWN OF GLORY

For those who fight to the end, there are rewards laid up in heaven, including a crown of glory. *2 Timothy 2:8 says Finally, there is laid up for me the crown of righteousness, which the Lord, the righteous Judge, will give to me on that Day, and not to me only but also to all who have loved His appearing.*

As a new believer, you must be heaven-focused and spiritually alert at all times, that you may fulfill your calling here on earth and in eternity, in Jesus' Name.

PRAYERS FOR EMPOWERMENT TO FINISH STRONG IN FAITH

WORSHIP DECREES
Let Your blood atone for me,
Let Your oil flow on my head
Let Your fire set my altars ablaze
Let Your wind blow over my soul
Let Your spirit fill me up
Let Your spirit be my companion

MEDIDATE
Revelation 21:22-27

> But I saw no temple in it, for the Lord God Almighty and the Lamb are its temple. The city had no need of the sun or of the moon to shine in it, for the glory of God illuminated it. The Lamb is its light. And the nations of those who are saved shall walk in its light, and the kings of the earth bring their glory and honor into it. Its gates shall not be shut at all by day (there shall be no night there). And they shall bring the glory and the honor of the nations into it. But there shall by no means enter it anything that defiles, or causes an abomination or a lie, but only those who are written in the Lamb's Book of Life.

PRAYER FOR PREPARATION TO FINISH WELL

1. My Lord, thank you for showing me deep and secret things in the name of Jesus.
2. In my journey with you, Lord do not allow me to be defeated in the name of Jesus
3. Spiritual sluggishness in not my portion in the name of Jesus
4. Spiritual slumber is not my portion in the name of Jesus
5. Barricade my life with your power in the name of Jesus
6. After my purpose is fulfilled on earth, I shall finish powerfully in the name of Jesus.
7. I shall not be derailed from the path of Christ in the name of Jesus
8. I shall not be lured out of my place in the Lord Jesus Christ in the name of Jesus.
9. I shall not be chased out of God's presence in the name of Jesus.
10. Iniquity shall not sneak into my life in the name of Jesus.
11. I shall not backslide in the name of Jesus
12. Lord, my life be preparation for eternity in the name of Jesus

9

~

1-Year Bible Study Plan for New Christians

This study plan is designed to help new believers build a strong foundation in their relationship with God. Each month focuses on a key theme, with weekly breakdowns for deeper study.

Month 1: The Basics of Salvation

Theme: Understanding what it means to be saved and follow Jesus.
- **Week 1:** What is the Gospel? (John 3:16, Romans 3:23, 6:23, 10:9-10)

- **Week 2:** Repentance and Faith (Acts 3:19, Ephesians 2:8-9)
- **Week 3:** Assurance of Salvation (1 John 5:11-13, Romans 8:1)
- **Week 4:** The New Life in Christ (2 Corinthians 5:17, Galatians 2:20)

Month 2: Knowing God Through His Word

Theme: The importance of Scripture and how to study it.
- **Week 1:** The Bible as God's Word (2 Timothy 3:16-17, Psalm 119:105)
- **Week 2:** How to Study the Bible (Joshua 1:8, Psalm 1:1-3)
- **Week 3:** The Power of Scripture (Hebrews 4:12, James 1:22-25)
- **Week 4:** Memorizing Key Verses (Psalm 119:11, Matthew 4:4)

Month 3: Prayer & Communion with God

Theme: Developing a strong prayer life.
- **Week 1:** The Lord's Prayer (Matthew 6:9-13)
- **Week 2:** Types of Prayer (Philippians 4:6-7, 1 Thessalonians 5:17)
- **Week 3:** Praying with Confidence (1 John 5:14-15, James 5:16)

- **Week 4:** Overcoming Prayer Challenges (Romans 8:26, Mark 11:24)

Month 4: The Holy Spirit & Spiritual Growth

Theme: Understanding the role of the Holy Spirit.
- **Week 1:** Who is the Holy Spirit? (John 14:16-17, Acts 1:8)
- **Week 2:** Fruits of the Spirit (Galatians 5:22-23)
- **Week 3:** Gifts of the Spirit (1 Corinthians 12:4-11)
- **Week 4:** Walking in the Spirit (Romans 8:5-6, Ephesians 5:18)

Month 5: Overcoming Sin & Temptation

Theme: Living in victory over sin.
- **Week 1:** The Nature of Sin (Romans 3:23, 1 John 1:8-9)
- **Week 2:** Resisting Temptation (1 Corinthians 10:13, James 4:7)
- **Week 3:** Forgiveness & Restoration (Psalm 51, 1 John 1:9)
- **Week 4:** Walking in Freedom (Romans 6:11-14, Galatians 5:1)

Month 6: The Church & Fellowship

Theme: The importance of Christian community.
- **Week 1:** What is the Church? (Matthew 16:18, Ephesians 2:19-22)
- **Week 2:** Why Fellowship Matters (Hebrews 10:24-25, Acts 2:42-47)
- **Week 3:** Serving in the Body of Christ (1 Peter 4:10, Romans 12:4-8)
- **Week 4:** Unity & Love Among Believers (John 13:34-35, 1 Corinthians 1:10)

Month 7: Sharing Your Faith

Theme: How to be a witness for Christ.
- **Week 1:** The Great Commission (Matthew 28:18-20)
- **Week 2:** Overcoming Fear in speaking about your faith to friends and family (Acts 1:8, 2 Timothy 1:7)
- **Week 3:** Practical Ways to Share Jesus with friends and family (1 Peter 3:15, Colossians 4:5-6)
- **Week 4:** Living as Salt & Light (Matthew 5:13-16)

Month 8: Trusting God in Trials

Theme: Finding strength in difficult times.
- **Week 1:** God's Sovereignty in Suffering (Romans 8:28, Jeremiah 29:11)
- **Week 2:** Persevering in Faith (James 1:2-4, 1 Peter 5:7)
- **Week 3:** God's Promises in Hard Times (Isaiah 41:10, Psalm 34:17-19)

- **Week 4:** Hope in Christ (Romans 15:13, 2 Corinthians 4:16-18)

Month 9: Living a Godly Life

Theme: Practical holiness in daily living.
- **Week 1:** Putting Off the Old Self (Ephesians 4:22-24, Colossians 3:5-10)
- **Week 2:** Honoring God in Work & Relationships (Colossians 3:23-24, 1 Thessalonians 4:3-5)
- **Week 3:** Managing Money Wisely (Proverbs 3:9-10, 1 Timothy 6:10)
- **Week 4:** Guarding Your Heart & Mind (Proverbs 4:23, Philippians 4:8)

Month 10: Worship & Gratitude

Theme: Cultivating a heart of worship.
- **Week 1:** What is True Worship? (John 4:23-24, Psalm 95:6)
- **Week 2:** Praise & Thanksgiving (Psalm 100, 1 Thessalonians 5:18)
- **Week 3:** Worship in Trials (Habakkuk 3:17-19, Acts 16:25)
- **Week 4:** Living a Life of Worship (Romans 12:1-2)

Month 11: The End Times & Christ's Return

Theme: Biblical prophecy and living with eternal perspective.

- **Week 1:** Signs of the Times (Matthew 24:4-14, 1 Thessalonians 5:1-6)
- **Week 2:** The Rapture & Second Coming (1 Thessalonians 4:16-17, Revelation 22:12)
- **Week 3:** Heaven & Eternal Life (John 14:1-3, Revelation 21:1-4)
- **Week 4:** Living with Urgency (2 Peter 3:10-13, Matthew 24:42-44)

Month 12: Discipleship & Growing Deeper

Theme: Maturing in faith and helping others grow.

- **Week 1:** The Cost of Discipleship (Luke 9:23-26, Matthew 16:24)
- **Week 2:** Abiding in Christ (John 15:1-8)
- **Week 3:** Mentoring Others (2 Timothy 2:2, Titus 2:3-5)
- **Week 4:** Continuing the Journey (Philippians 3:12-14, Hebrews 12:1-2)

NOTES

ABOUT THE AUTHORS

Ebenezer Gabriels is an Innovator, Apostle of the Lord Jesus, the Apostle of Worship, Innovation Leader, Prophetic Leader, Revivalist, and a Computer Scientist who has brought heaven's solutions into Financial markets, Technology, and Government with his computational gifts. Apostle Ebenezer Gabriels is anointed as a Prophetic Leader of nations with the mantle of healing, worship music, national deliverance, foundational deliverance, complex problem-solving, and building Yahweh's worship altars.

Abigail Ebenezer-Gabriels, a Teacher, Business Leader, Strategy and Policy Expert, Executive Co-Founder at the Ebenezer Gabriels Teacher, Worshiper, and Multi-disciplinary leader in Business, Technology, Education, and Development. Blessed with prophetic teaching abilities, with the anointing to unveil the mysteries in the Word of God. She is a Multi-specialty Keynote Speaker, with a special anointing to explain Heaven's ordinances on earth.

Ebenezer Gabriels & Abigail Ebenezer-Gabriels are married, and building worship altars for the Lord across industries.

www.ingramcontent.com/pod-product-compliance
Lightning Source LLC
Chambersburg PA
CBHW032216040426
42449CB00005B/623